Star Lake
Arda Collins

The Song Cave

The Song Cave
www.the-song-cave.com
Cover image © *Two Plant Specimens*, by William Henry Fox Talbot, 1839.

Design and layout by Janet Evans-Scanlon

ISBN: 978-1-7372775-4-5
Library of Congress Control Number: 2021952576

FIRST EDITION

For Bryan

Contents

Far-Off Day

There's a castle in the distance yonder,
like the poem of a third grader
imagining medieval ways.
A fence with spear points coming out of dead vines on the castle wall,
low horizon stones
blue and gray, branches
after rain, light in the sky
across a field.
It's a stately,
time-free point on a dimension.
Your eyes, your voice,
you, as I would say to me,
and you who are you
who are mine.
Give away,
slide down a river to a railway;
come to time.

John Maloney

John Maloney said his uncle owns a giraffe. He owns a giraffe, he said, because his uncle owns a zoo. "He's rich," he said in a tone of beatific concentration, as though he was pouring water into a stream from a jug and imagining that others grasped for his attention. "He's rich," he continued. Our desks were next to each other's and we had to share glue. John Maloney became a handyman. My mother said, "Do you remember John Maloney? He came by here and gave us his card. He's a handyman now. He was very sweet. He's having a baby. Kheghj pan." "Kheghj pan" is Armenian for "this person, he inspires pathos in me." She died of cancer in her bed in the house where she lived for forty-seven years. It was a modest ranch where she had known great love. On the piano, she was learning Franz Liszt's composition "Love Dream." The day she died she went on an inquiry that began, "Are you blue?" She asked the question in many ways, appeared to listen as an answer came, and spoke again. Downtown in the village, the waves in the harbor were choppy from the wind in the bright sun. Later that night she was still, then lavender as she changed. I knelt by her bed in an unfamiliar dark and felt frightened this was all there would be. In the morning, the air in the room was full. Particles were visible and turned in the sun. It was soft like sediment, and metallic, like blood becoming light, and a knife in a dream and the dream disappears. In its place is a live meadow. The meadow pulls apart as the day moves.

Wuthering Heights

I need to play this small blue saxophone.
It's been moldering in my cousin's basement,
transposed in my mind
as my childhood basement,
for many years. It was gnawed and spit in
by at least seven Armenian children,
my cousins, who, like me, sprang from the women
driven from their homes
while their husbands and fathers were seized and murdered. Over time
we appeared. Every note
is like a pothole when I think of the day
I couldn't control myself
and blew in it. I felt a passing knowledge
something else would happen.
Then thunder and a rainstorm.
It was like opening a book.
All the stories I read took place
in versions of my old house. Since then,
I've lived in a number of houses
and have been inside so many others,
who can remember them? There are houses
I've seen in movies, and suggestions
of houses in drawings and plays. "In the Hall of the Mountain King"
is about a house, and *The Nutcracker*

takes place in a house
that leads to a forest in an endless
kingdom filled with sweets, flowers,
and melancholy spirits. This morning,
I started reading a novel. The setting
is a rocky shore. Inside
the stone house where the protagonist lives
there is a version
of a kitchen that belonged to my childhood friend
when her family lived in a Victorian manse. I continue
to invoke this place,
mostly the neutral side driveway entrance
outside the living room porch. Woods
and a cemetery beyond them
lead to a small lawn around the house
that is part of a larger lawn
bordered by pine trees
with a somber, military bearing.
It's the initial staging area
for confusing memories. I recognized
a weeknight mood of their kitchen
in the story about the rocky coast: "This reminds you
of that," I thought. Then the protagonist stood at the wooden counter
in the kitchen where I live now.
"She's chopping vegetables, like you,"
my mind said. All day my mind
worked, showing me pictures

of feelings it had retrieved

from the world

and from inside of me. "Who are you?"

I asked. My mind showed me

the small wooded area

beyond my backyard

where mud and leaves marked the tracks

of a seasonal stream.

Then there was the grass

in March, the ground frozen; dormant

growth in the trees; rocks locked away

inside the earth; sky after sky,

this one

gray, another light blue,

a rainy October night,

February twilight,

a time I thought the sun was loud. This poem

is called "Wuthering Heights"

because the house in that novel is an ongoing

contraption of consciousness,

time, and space. Now can we

be together?

Late Summer, Late Winter, and Genocide

Jump in a skirt
in a fright,
jump in the ocean, tormented by pleasure.
A fountain would tumble around you, and when this would happen,
imagine a star without tethers.
All there is is forever,
an apricot tree and stones in the dust, the edge of your soul at your face.

A war happens
far from you, and inside
your face is where it lies. The sky is blue
and all its corollaries have only ever been that

                        your family of refugees is eventually free.

The nameplate from the mailbox, a jewelry watch in the back of a drawer.
Your great-grandmother carried her children
across the desert, your grandmother, her sister, their brother
who died,
your mother, her sister,
their brother who died,

you, your sister;
weren't you at this?

Didn't we survive someday? You, you eat marshmallow candy and
       coffee for breakfast
and swelter at work serving fish at a bar. Keep your heart light
or keep it full of sorrow; it's been decades since I started this poem
and now it's tomorrow.
Low thunder in a purple sky scares the horses. Chert fossils
from an old ocean scatter in the desert covered over with dirt.

                         The river is distended
                         with the bodies of dead Armenians.

The sun is on the mountains at the train.
You wake up, and to a day

that won't be excavated. A striated February sky
one day won't be a mystery to you
or there won't be another day
for it to be a mystery to you.
Large over the snow
day comes
into midstreet sunlight; we're the dark!
We're the dark,
and it's far
to another star,
to light only inches away,
to anywhere.
Even the air here,
we go up in walking,
so lighthearted are we.

From a June Sky

Beati, rex tremendae
majestatis,
gigantic flowers come to morning gratis
in paradise.
Climbed the lattice and slept.
A little yellow window
above the alley,
a wait to be interred.
You get a handle on it,
it's piety.
You came here through the garage
and ambled in the way;
ambulant in lege Domini.

Wind

Where is the poem?
The wind is the poem!
I spend the day carefully.
At night, the night sky
comes in; past skies follow. Cold wind,
night wind, white wind,
blue wind, snow wind, slight wind,
black wind, tight wind,
light wind, new wind; ocean clouds
above the grassy March shore; darkness
pulls over the water
through the yard
into the trees, a formation
like the remainder
of a mountain.
The mountain comes
through my mind
each night,
my mind a small valley
near a small sea. I fall asleep
to wind noises.
I don't know why
I make them. In the dark,
swirls, upturns,

and atonal refrains. I'm much better
at this
than the flute. These
are the original
versions of myself before I was me. I was not
nothing; I was so many things—
a shell, a peacock's
tongue, a bend in the road, a dot
of blood, mica,
a seed, a sound—
that my life could be
a continuous effort
to know them all.

Arda,
my dad said
from my head.
His selves through time
are stored
in a multidimensional vault
so he can appear. *Arda,*
you should write a poem
about the wind.
I was already doing that!
Why should he
be here?

Pretending this was his
idea! He wanted to be
the lead in the poem
so the wind would be
him instead of wind.
Get out of here!
I said
in my thoughts
but not with my voice.
Why say a hurtful thing
to a dead person? A reverberation
came to call. A resilient
presence projected
through a vestibule in my mind
I can't comprehend, vast
and miniscule. All day in the rain
I scrambled
from sidewalk to sidewalk.
Full of sorrow,
I lumbered
and wandered past dark
looking for rest;
I walked until
my clothes were in tatters
and the ocean was still.

Summer Day

The trees and sunshine
and sky in the quiet town
where I live. Here
at the main intersection, this kind of summer day
reminds me of driving
and loneliness;
I'm grateful to still be myself.
Last week
was the last
time I'll ever
see my father's
brother, a presence
of my father
before me. In the sky,
sun, and trees, there is
silence. I tell them everything. "It's a June green afternoon,
darker within the leaves."
They know everything about me
because I've told them,
with my eyes,
for many years. I have more to say
but I'm at the post office and I have to go home now.

Story

Early mist after sleep.
Another time, sunlight like an immense, bright hole.
I bend in the soil.
One day the wind comes through
the leaves' pale undersides,
like every type of thought.
Night is a story
where we can reside in a story.
Outside the night
there is no story.

Wish, Swish

A butterfly appears
out of the corner of your eye.
Somewhere, there is a painting.
A full sky, a face
pointed up, an angel
with a golden aura
pops out from one corner.
You do,
it comes in,
the mammoth particulate reality,
blood stationed everywhere
under a lignite sundown. A freight
of light, peat, ash;
an ocean, blue, like you.
A door chimes,
parietal, galactic,
inside a skull or two.

Medieval Love Poem and Time Travel

A black shadow,
my soul is on the floor. A lost earring
by the pillow under sunrise;
come in the window.
An orange in the dark
is like lake air at night;
it's one way to a planet.
The ocean rests
with sea pebbles in a pile by its side
after rain. A meteor
above in the night.
Trees cast down shadows
like a lake in the grass.

Wake in bed and the air is gray;
spring might stay.
What do you feel
from far away?
Morning says
a far away feeling
is here to stay.

Milk, a wolf, coal,
flowers, and landscape paintings. Night at the table

and in the summer leaves. You'll be gone forever!
The way summer leaves.

In the past, they smoked ham in hay.
If they didn't sleep through the night
they got up, worked, fed the animals,
talked, and lay there.

The grass is like licorice,
nothing is a replica.

Tonight on the pommel horse
you rose over a mountain. Jupiter
sends back every minute that fails,
to do it all again one day.

To the sunset, pole vault over a palm frond!
Inaudible love, I don't know
the pines in a rainstorm.

Early

The shells are on,
we are billowing.
The white inside
curves under the sky.
We're in a gray
and whitened day
horizontal to the air.
It reminds me of a little while
that's almost nothing.
It's not like anything;
the white in the branches
is near and low. Abalone rainbow;
life billows out
tomorrow, a swirling heart
invisible again.
Night,
what you look like,
blue iridescent
mother of pearl;
morning sun between the pines'
black lines; an atom in a shadow; a lake through the trees.
Rings on the water open
how I hear.

Love

I read a story I thought was written by a baby. It was not. It was written by an adult woman who had failed to see the logic in her life. It was critical of many things. At some point in the story, she ate at a restaurant in the evening with a friend. The autumn sun was setting near the window where they sat and she admitted to love. No one threw stones at her but she saw in the pink and orange sky, and the dark, ashen clouds, that her admission was right and she would pay for it. Everyone else said they loved freely with an open heart, or not at all, or whatever it was that made them exceptional.

Air

My longing for you is like clouds,
the coming motion
the day's events together.
It's heaven.
Brick under the pale,
mandible blue
winter we're in. There is no reflecting
the gold singular upward
mirror building windows;
ursine sunset,
metal-rose hue,
sunset coming
and coming away.
Walking more than one dusk
to walk into the one
that arrives
with a postal ring not yet
reached my ears.
Wail, pale, and sail.
I shoot myself in the face,
a kiss I heard your thought through,
and catch up.

September October

How many centuries equal gold pennies?
How many?
How many?
How many?
Suns or days
of fallen-down light?
Tossed, the stream
in the small woods
follows a plane of pebbles underwater
hundreds of years into the sun.
A soft day
on the banks where trees had fallen. Humid sunlight
after a storm. A new time set in.
Evening cools and smoothes.
Who is a penny in the river?
Who is a shiny rock?
Who is the water and who is the light?
A shiver, a love, one you miss, and a wish.
Where the riverbed is shallow
look in; pain shines, scatters, fades, and goes far away,
now driving a car on a parkway into sundown.

Old Snow

I miss you so much
waking, whisper to you,
dead;
it won't ever be
enough
and can't know
just how dead;
separated this morning
by the window and the bed,
where is dead?
I see it when I see you.

My Mother's Face

Is this going to be a serious poem?
A sad one?
Should we run?
A poem of tribute?
A poem of tribute and complaint?
Of anguish?
A jubilant expression
of filial love?
A sentimental dirge
that descends into rage
at the incomprehensibility of it all?
A tender breeze through the garden in early spring,
the first soft day.
My mother's face,
I love it.
I can't show it to you.
This is a poem,
not a picture.
I refuse to describe it to you.
I refuse to tell anyone about her.
I will keep writing and you might keep reading
because both of us are hoping
I will describe it.
Her face is an oval.

The poem

could have begun,

"Is there anything I love to look at more?"

Her eyes are gone.

Her whole face is gone.

Where is it?

Her face is ashes now.

I am afraid

a very strict rule

will come out from somewhere

that says, "Now that your mother is dead,

you're no longer permitted to imagine her face. Once a face is gone,

it is gone forever." I will have this argument

in my mind, under a blanket

on a light gray afternoon

exactly like my mother's face.

For my whole childhood

I feared

sunny days in January.

The orange light

told me

this is my mother's death.

I tried to forget.

How elegant

and odd

to see a wide beam

move through the bare trees

for an hour,
and a pink sunset
over last week's snow.
"Where are you?"
I said.
A house
where a body lies
dead through the night
in the morning
is full of bizarre
air and sound. In the quiet
you can hear outside
of reality. It's loud,
like the vibrations in a warehouse
or the vault of sound in the sky
from an airplane. The atoms of light
make a massive noise; I can't hear it;
I see it in the yard and the street
through the kitchen window. Something beyond
the air occurs. My mind is there with it.
My mother's eyes are large.
Now do you know what she looks like?
She has wide eyelids and dark eyelashes.
Her eyebrows are black and round.
Her irises are light brown
on the axis of the winter sun.

I saw her face
like she was a statue.
She was asleep
under anesthesia
in a fancy hospital bed
that she won
in an outlandish lottery
conducted by the hospital.
The room was like a hotel.
Her face was in total
repose, without even the machinations
of sleep. She was outside of time.
I didn't know such a face of anyone
was possible. My father,
who could be cruel, looked something like this
in the first moments
he was gone.

Walk the Days

1

The lakes are behind
the shadows; deer at night
quick in the grass and snow.

2

Brittle, there is electricity
in the ice. It breaks in the sun,
then the day is dark
over the road and rocks.

3

You're someplace.
In another solar system
there's a blue sky
and wheat or snow
blow to one side.

A lake as dark
as a mirror
in the dark. An ocean
tide goes out
to the unlit origin.

4

You startle
and think of Saturn.
You wish for vivid
grassland, green like a diamond.
Madness
blows through you
descending a hill
into vertices and voids.

5

A star comes through the pond
in the black, shallow water,
a mirror bounding in eternity,
a wish
outside of it.

6

A star, a remnant
of a star, comes to a pond
and fills it. The star is wide.
It's a cadence repository.

7

Morning
reaches into kelp under the black waves.

The sun bright brown and blue
on a hazel thistle returns the ocean to the day.
It's the time of day
the light changes over. The bottom of the slopes
ring to an inlet; sunset
is white at the end,
like a bone, before night.

8

It's 6:22.
The dim
closes in the lamplight
across the dark hall—
eons come in close:
in one note
they're still, they're here; they move,
it's us.

9

They bent down
the two hounds
they made they became
the branches and lake
snow on the road that bends that would end.

10

In one of the afterlives,
walking up the road
bored and afraid.
It's freezing out,
your own breath
over the brown leaves.

11

What you had recognized
is lost. The sun
is out and winds up a dirt trail
in the grass that gets narrow and goes higher
up from life.

12

The fence in the grass buckles
under rain; clouds advance
in a shallow sky
over a field
that used to be water.

Scale

A cloud is big. The shadow of a cloud on a mountain is big. A small cloud is still large. You can dig a hole to plant an apple tree or a hole deep enough to find water, but a hole that releases molten rock would be as big as a volcano. You know you're at the beach because the landscape, the expanse of sand and rocks and the view of the water under the sky, surrounds you. You have to sit on top of a log though, or stand very close, for it to be a place in its own right; otherwise the log is part of a larger setting. You can't go inside an anthill or between the ridges of bark on a tree, or sleep inside a flower like an insect. These places are small and always very far away, and so you can't go there. You would have to use a microscope to see the details of these things, the way you would use opera glasses to see the emotion in the singers' faces or a telescope to see the surface of the moon.

Last night I laughed so hard at a TV show that it turned into uncontrollable weeping. It was agony and there was a silver darkness in my mind. The silver darkness had once been far away, so that before, I could only imagine it, and now it was very close and I could see it inside my head. It was so near it was as though the great darkness of the night and beyond the Earth was there, and in it was an X-ray of a rock or the profile of a beloved lying beside me. Once when I was ten, I went with my mother to a church in a nearby town to hear a choir sing Maurice Duruflé's Requiem. The church was made of stone and had a solemn presence in the middle of a busy downtown street. It was a cloudy day in the summer and I was in good spirits, though I knew where we were going. As soon as the soloist began to sing the high notes of "Pie Jesu," I began to laugh, but silently. I silently laughed so hard, I was doubled over and covering my face with my hands. My mother became worried, that my laughing would disturb the concert but also about what was happening to me. She decided we should leave. I was afraid she would be angry but she wasn't. In the car, I sat in the back without speaking and my legs stretched out on the seat. As she drove, her expression showed that she was both asking a question and knew she was the answer to it. When we got home, it was only four-thiry. I lied down in my clothes, on my bed still made, and wept into the darkness in space. It was like the first time I saw an El Camino. One drove past the window and I laughed so hard at the shape of this car speeding up the street I thought I might start screaming. Where is my mother? Is she near or far? Like a neutrino or like a moon? A whale I imagine, or the white air over the pond on a summer evening?

Nothing

Lightning over the field
out of the voltage in the atmosphere
spins the grass in a thunder wash.
The metallic light
outlines a mineral rain
that smells like ashes
and purple clover.
Like a day of old sun,
you can hardly believe the world is still here
under the auspices of an afternoon
with eternity on the perimeter.
A slab of an invisible, wide force
makes you envision your parents' burial
under a two-way cloud.
In the wet grass
the sky lightens.

Thursday

Don't ever say anything.

We don't die once but many times.
Death is long
and changes—
we won't be nearly
as dead
at the beginning
as after—

All along in the grass,
heat; the damp spring air
spirals to the ball-peen sun.
The stream here
lies with the past
so no embrace will be forgotten
or a shout
born from its course
lost into light.

Awake with a start;
time comes through a face like a star.

In the day, each filament of air full of sun
exits down to evening, like remembering
something a painting
told you one time:

The light you see here
is the light as it was.

It's the last sky of the day.
Rain splits the night back.

Way

Of its place,
the low stream.
I fail at seeing
and at everything. The small sun
blinds, orange at three
through winter on the field.
I'm open in the air
and around the water;
limpets on the shale, shade by a pond,
that's an expression
told to me by the matter
that comprises everything. It's a literal translation
of the idiom, "The snail arrived in paradise."
A nothing blooms
by the white sun gray
stones, but yes,
I've never seen those,
I say to all.
Oversimplification could make meat out of you.
The late afternoon is white and sheer. It is an elbow.
We are melted.
It's as if I'm looking at an encircled field
at the back of my head.
But I'm not because it's right there.
His eyes roll back in his head.

Shaded Road

My life seems short and uninteresting
but I like it.
Oh, this is something only I see,
my mind's short hop
back to where I had been,
a young, smiling, rounded face,
lonely and afraid.
Really though,
where am I?
A spool of thread,
the garden in the alley, evening,
dim as it courses
through my ears,
blood from stars.

Love in Another Dimension

The drapes on the congress of light scale out the city.

No magic broken or taken away.

It isn't any longer,

we're just longer.

Hop to the bed to fort the happiness;

winter stills the lake shore.

Of course I love you!

Down the boulevard,

past cement pillars in horizon rain,

Versailles is everywhere.

112

Life is fucking hard,
a pond that turns
darker, the world over, a forest
turns red. You are so
strangely in my purpose bred.
I sucked on your tongue
while your blood
told me something,

a wild accident.
Green without starlight,
what's sore, you understand.

I wince and burn
and go
back to what's left.

I hear your voice
and nothing is mine.
In a dream about wild flowers,
I saw
that I'm mostly soil,
blooms

like a plink on a piano
along a riverbank.

Winter smoke
hovers and remains.
No one else;
what's inside me, my tongue, your tongue
the world
in that heat.
All this talk is making me grieve.

It was mild
in your prose lows woes.

You seem to see
no light and no shadow, no ray anywhere, not at all like
a sunset, neglect, not a pond, not stars burning, not a white moon burnt
and hidden in shimmers.
Through this, I love you and true,
there are ways
that must be;
a kiss on the forelock
for the horse at the doorstep;
at the end of the story
all that is said
is quickly redressed and put into bed.

Wild Love

F.P., I am in love with you beyond anything I can imagine. The azaleas on my street in the spring, the stones in the garden, or the end of the driveway. Not nearly anything can make me love the way I do when I'm with you and we sit next to each other at school. I think about you in the tree where I sit in the afternoons and I can love you, though I cannot imagine who you are. You are filled with contempt, but I don't know that. I remember a forest near an ocean where I listened for the sound of God ready to speak to me. It took so long I thought it might never happen. I slept near the water and God was in the morning air. I do not love F.P. I drew a heart around our initials in my diary once, so long ago, but I didn't mean it anymore. I sat on a forested dune on an island at the bottom of the world. Here, I mourned my dead before they were gone. Next, I saw in a pocked stone the man who raped me. I went into the forest by a manuka tree. In this rape, we were inside an invisible black wind. I focused on the forest until he disappeared. In the morning, the air through the car window blew into my forehead and told me what to do. I left the carcass of this rape by a pine tree, who told another pine tree, etc. By the river where I live there is a pine tree and a willow tree together. They directed me about the afterlife. My parents were dead. I drove past the pine tree and the willow tree and came through the sensation of eternity that had taken hold of me, and the knowledge that the end of my life might never end. One day, there was a man, another man, and another man. They are my sons. Their father came out of the ocean and I said to him, "I love them with wild love."

Afternoon

Now we're on a big, flat, sunny road
by the grocery store.
It's cold enough outside.
We can't believe it,
how we're here together;
then we talk about eternity
when the whole thing is, is
we're already in it: this
is eternity. *The air*
doesn't separate us
from anything. "So what's different
about death?" we ask
each other. Who else
can tell us? The day in the windshield
is very close. Your head turned
towards me
shows a distant ecstasy.
On a blue evening
the snow melts. The branches
are dark and wet,
or a wind blows over us,
metaphor after metaphor,
and you appear
from nowhere each day.

Middle Distance

May,
this is a particular day of the Earth
that's a model
of what life is.
A didactic ghost intoned that from inside my mind:
a tiny fossil, one of my parents,
someone,
familiar to me though
unidentified, from the ongoing exchange of quiet
between my mind and the world all around.
I could say, "I'm tired of being haunted"
as though life is glamorous.
Listen to me,
I implore in silence.
I mean it though,
and what I mean is be with me forever
because forever is all we have.
In a dusty field at the edge of the lot
by the doctor's office
there are a few trees at the far edge
and some low buildings.
An afternoon wind blows.
May green shines
through the sun. Is this

what life is? It's *like*
this? What does life
resemble? Another life
we remember? I might be anything.
The past and the future
in my feelings
move cohesively today. I can feel this
as I feel my original sight inside me.
"I think I have something for us today," I say.
I feel through my eyes
and look out at the view.
I write in my journal
(there is no journal),
Last night my son had a fever.
I want him to get well.
My children have been with me all my life, unseen,
just as I rode along
with my mother through her life,
going places and doing things, while set apart
from human affairs.
At the edge of this precipice
our being is laid out
as the trees move. The world
is familiar but not known.
The recess they came from
is in their eyes, a wide place
with an interior I've seen.

Ghosts

I went to the eye doctor because I sometimes saw a flash in the corner of my eye. The flash looked like it had been painted by a clever, boring artist. It was a little, glowing painting that descended quickly down my peripheral vision. This painting was a splatter made to resemble a light bulb partially obscured by darkness. The clever part was that the light bulb seemed to suggest that it was actually supposed to be a lemon. This was a tacit joke among the three of them: the artist, the light bulb, and the lemon.

The eye nurse asked me some questions. Then she put numbing drops in my eyes, and then other drops that dilated my pupils. She left and I waited for the doctor. I knew the eye drops weren't meant to make you drowsy, but I became sleepy while I waited. Everything looked blurry and large, like a true version of the world.

The doctor came in and we spoke a bit while she looked inside my eye. Then she put down her instrument and said, "There's nothing wrong with your retina. It's ghosts." "What ghosts?" I asked her. "Any ghosts," she said. "Do you know any? They could be in there. Their particles." I had suspected this but I was surprised it could be a medical diagnosis. "We don't always say this to patients, but since you're a physicist I thought you would understand," she told me. I appreciated her candor. I waited by the vending machine until my pupils returned to normal.

August

August,
no one can do anything about it.
The sunlight is made of sorrow.
There's a shadow
under the arbor
at the Blessing of the Grapes
church picnic someplace,
an invisible facet of the world
inside the multitudinous shade. Gray smoke
rises over the sunlight, the ash
of roasting meat.
My veins are lavender;
I'm anxious in the sun,
then under the leaves.
I didn't know
there was a day
on its way
from this light
when my eye socket
would be broken
by a full moon
that got too close.
One August afternoon
I walked past a black walnut tree

with my broken eye;
a walnut just like my eye!
like I'd found a penny
on the ground,
or my old eye.
I prayed as though God
was inside
as I skipped down the street
with the walnut
and I thought,

Let's face it,
our dreams are an attempt
by the bacteria
that fabricate our insides
to communicate with us. If we eat
"a fragment
of an underdone potato,"
like Ebenezer Scrooge, and then
have a bad dream in which
several real ghosts
appear, we could
blame the potato, or
accept our cells'
earnest message
regarding the future. "Who
is Ebenezer Scrooge?" you might be asking.

You might be

only four

years old or

not human, possibly

a ghost

of a fern, a stone, the spirit

of an apple

blossom. Reader, you

are in the future

of the August afternoon

I'm in now. I remember

my fear yesterday,

swimming across the pond. In the middle

I saw deep water

all around, and nothing

near. I was nowhere.

There were branches under the sky.

I cried out

and my heart unwound

a part of me

towards the air. Now

I'm here

and can say this and that,

mark the light I see,

my insides a dark corridor

of blood where a thought

comes to be. You may be

gone. If you can't

read because now

there is only starlight

left to read,

then goodbye, I love you!

And if you don't know

the story called "A Christmas Carol"

by the nineteenth-century

author Charles Dickens, then, like Scrooge,

you may think to yourself

about me, "You may be

an undigested

bit of beef,

a blot

of mustard,

a crumb of cheese,

a fragment

of an underdone potato. There's more

of gravy

than of grave about you,

whatever you are!"

Elegy from Space

The sun is death.
Land burns
into a shade of vision.
A pancreas, a liver
flower up a piece of time.
The desert is nothing.
Corpses
decompose into shadows.
Today, from space
someone could see
a cheetah squint in the sun.
Gloss of the blue sky
bows against the infinite,
if it is infinite,
like a glistening arrow
or a blistering light.

Restored Ending

I love this
when it's not tragedy
inverted. *A Winter's Tale*
is not what I have in mind. The lifelike
statue of the queen, the return
of the others,
is meant to hurt
you more than the original loss. The end is a wish,
which is terrible; wishes
come from sorrow. What I'm looking for
is fantastical:
the protagonist wins
the town field-day race,
finishes a breath-
taking dance, an unimaginable
garden is revealed, finally
you have passed the test. The villains are vanquished,
become gracious and clap. Everyone
you've ever loved is there. All that was
too diffuse
to comprehend
is now apprehensible.

I still can't believe the ending
of this book
isn't what I thought
it was going to be. There was that time
I drove past a pine tree and a willow tree
under a rift in the winter sky
and I didn't know I
screamed until
the sound was almost over. The trees
were my parents; the trees were spirits
among many others; the trees spoke;
they stood in repose; the willow tree
had cancer, just like my mother,
and the pine tree was angry about it
like my father and pointed a branch
toward me and the sky, pointed to
his anger, pointed to something I couldn't see, a gesture
of counsel. The pine tree and the willow tree
are in love, together by the river,
singing at the piano, talking about
old songs, my father excited about a novel he read,
both of them playing down being dead.
The world is a very sophisticated place.
There are a lot of leaves at the sides of the road.

This Is the Poem

An illustration of a peach
that says peach at the bottom;
the Armenian word for "bed,"
"angoghin," which means something more
like a large cradle that flies
out into a dream or a dark
sleep; several driveways after it rained
in places I've lived; made-up scenes
of oceans and savannahs;
late winter with a damp white sky,
God nearby; the time I wanted to jump straight through
my black mind.
Put your cheek
against an animal's fur. Tell me what you think about
the different kinds of light
you saw today. You can give them names.
You can hear the end
of time right here inside this cloud,
where there's a tube of lightning,
a miniscule
revolving echo,
like a drive through a tunnel.

Easter

It feels like any other day,
my aunt commented from the steering wheel,
my mother in the front seat,
my sister and I in the back.
It was a warm spring afternoon
and unusually empty
going down Second Avenue.
A cab bumped along and floated
as it sped ahead of us.

What can I relay
from here, a winter morning
far in the future
from then? The winter day I'm writing this,
sitting on the bed getting dressed,
will also be in the past.
The Easter in my head
is there as though
it's in the room,
like hearing the forested road outside
through the window.

We drove home from church.
There was hardly anybody
on Queens Boulevard. It was sunny
and there was one person on the median
and someone else farther away
selling flowers
from a bucket
inside the light of the afternoon
near a car dealership and a nightclub. My grandmother
and great-aunt were waiting for us at home
with lamb and pilaf, Armenian Easter.
They didn't go to church
because they had survived the genocide. I wondered
if God was around. I leaned into the back seat
window. The dress I wore was like
a costume, but I didn't know. It was pink with a sailor
collar, made from a pattern
in my grandmother's basement.
I had on white patent leather
Mary Janes with ankle socks. I didn't know
how old I was (eleven)
was quite old
for these clothes. Was I
a baby again? The year before, I had worn
an appropriate dress. It was as though I had run out
of childhood and had nowhere to go
except to being a child in a cartoon or a play. I had gone

back to the beginning where I was no longer
real. My sister had recently
cut off all my hair
while she was upset
and my father pushed me across the room—
I felt air under my feet as I blew
through a doorway—
when I complained about a book
and other things.

Excuse me,
I'd like to write about something else.
I saw the most wonderful foreign movie
two years ago. It was called *Autumnal*.
I'm surprised I liked it
because I'd never heard of it. My name is Barbara.
I'm from Long Island but I've lived in Sudbury,
MA for many years. It's about a young woman and her brother
whose father is a sculptor. He's dying
and wants to leave a piece of his work
to a cellist with whom he's been in love for many years.
The young woman's mother is dead. Her brother
is actually the son of the cellist
but none of them know this. *Autumnal*
is the name of the sculpture. It's very valuable. It's of a man
expiring in a pile of leaves while a woman
gives birth and a robed figure stands nearby. There's a dispute

and it ends where

the sculpture is donated to the convent

where the cellist had left the son

when he was born. In the last scene,

the cellist, the sister, and the brother walk through an autumn field.

November Afternoon

was the original title. I told my sons to watch it.

I don't know if they did.

I have three sons: Michael, David, and Greg.

Michael and David work with computers

and Greg works for a medical technology

company. My husband is half Italian and half Czech. I'm

half Armenian, half Greek. We just visited our friends

in Westchester and the traffic is terrible.

We're not going to get home until very late.

Acknowledgments

Grateful acknowledgment is made to the editors of the publications in which earlier versions of these poems have appeared: *A Public Space, Colorado Review, Fonograf, Iowa Review, jubilat, The Map of Every Lilac Leaf: Poets Respond to the Smith College Museum of Art,* ed. Matt Donovan, *The Sonnets: Translating and Re-Writing Shakespeare,* ed. Sharmila Cohen and Paul Legault, and *Washington Square Review.*

This book was made possible, in part, with the support of fellowships from Yaddo and the University of Denver.

Thank you to Ben Estes and Alan Felsenthal for their guidance, and for all that The Song Cave does.

Notes

"From a June Sky" uses lyrics from "Beati quorum via," from Charles Villiers Stanford's *Three Latin Motets,* and Mozart's Requiem in D Minor.

The title "September October" is based on the title of the film *October November,* directed by Götz Spielmann.

"112" uses Shakespeare's "Sonnet 112" as its starting point.

OTHER TITLES FROM THE SONG CAVE: